MOMMY, THIS IS NOT A GOOD IDEA!

WRITTEN BY
FALILATOU GHAUM-BAUDA

First published in 2022

Written by Falilatou GHAUM-BAUDA

ISBN: 979-8-9869853-1-2 (paperback edition)
ISBN: 979-8-9869853-0-5 (hardcover edition)

To my beloved mom

iT'S A BIG DAY FOR GEORGE. He's going to be a big brother.

Baby brother will be his playmate. George will help baby brother fight monsters, play games, sing songs and watch his favorite cartoons.

George will be the **BEST OLDER BROTHER EVER.**

Mommy has been at the hospital. In a few moments,

Mommy and Daddy will come home with a newborn baby.

DING DONG!

"They are here!" says Grandma.

The door opens. Mommy looks tired but happy. Daddy is carrying bags.

BUT WHERE IS BABY BROTHER?

"Here he is, George," says Mommy.
She leans down and shows George the **TINY BUNDLE** in her arms.

The baby's face is **SMALLER THAN A DOLL'S.**

His ears are like tiny seashells.

His feet could fit in a postage stamp.

"But why is he **SO SMALL?**" asks George, feeling confused.

"He doesn't look like a baby brother."

The baby doesn't sing; he screams. He also smells nasty.

And even though he doesn't do much, he gets a
WHOLE LOT OF LOVE from Mommy and Daddy.

"Mommy, do you think this is a good idea?" asks George.

"Maybe I don't need a baby brother after all."

Mommy and Daddy laugh.

"He still a baby," they say. "In time, you will love him."

GEORGE IS NOT SO SURE.

George walks through the door and accidentally knocks over a vase.

Baby brother starts screaming.

Baby brother is **CRANKY.**

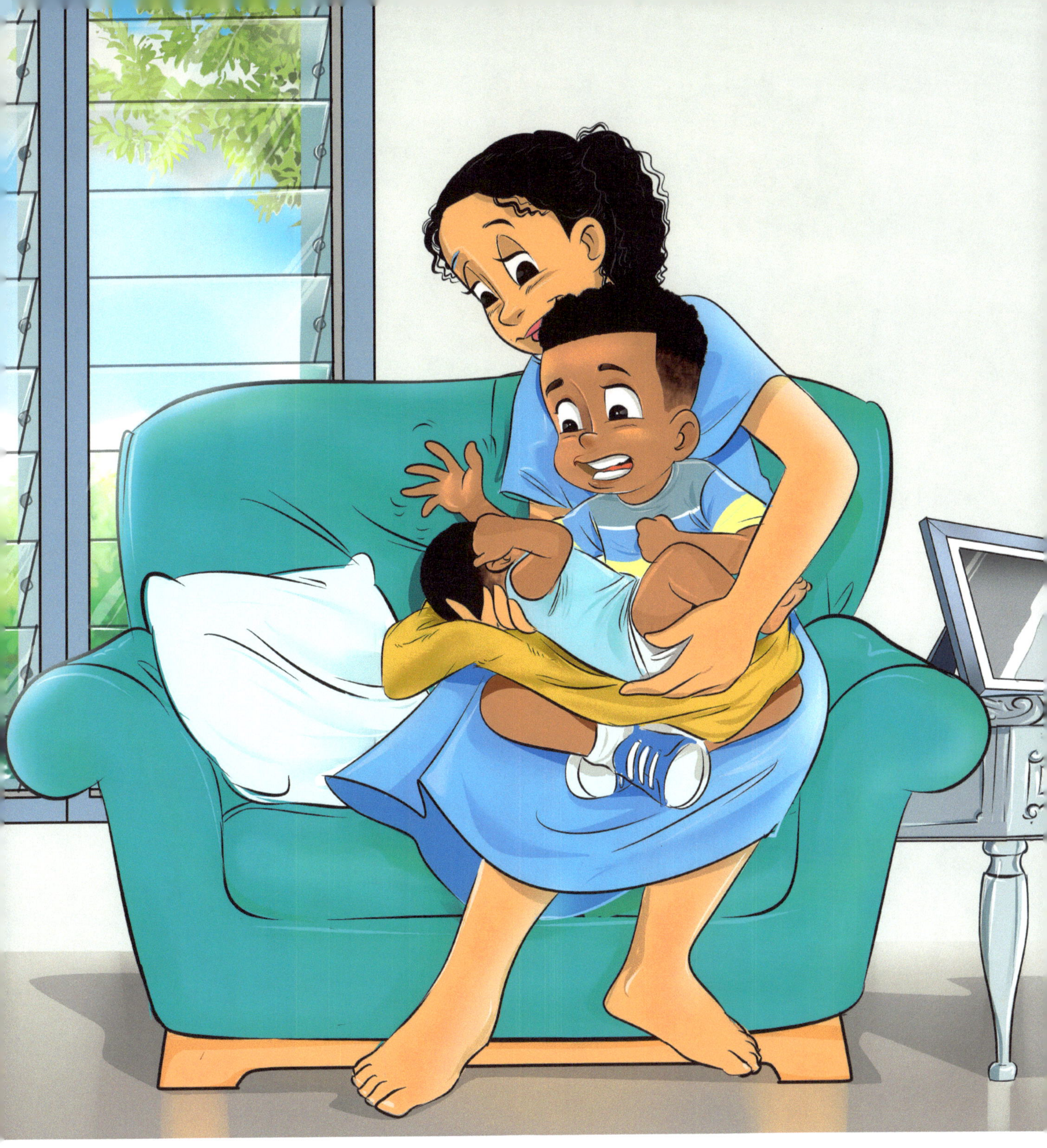

When George wants a cuddle,
Mommy is **BUSY** holding the baby.

GEORGE MUST WALK,
but baby brother can ride in the new stroller.

George wants **To sing,**

but baby brother is sleeping.

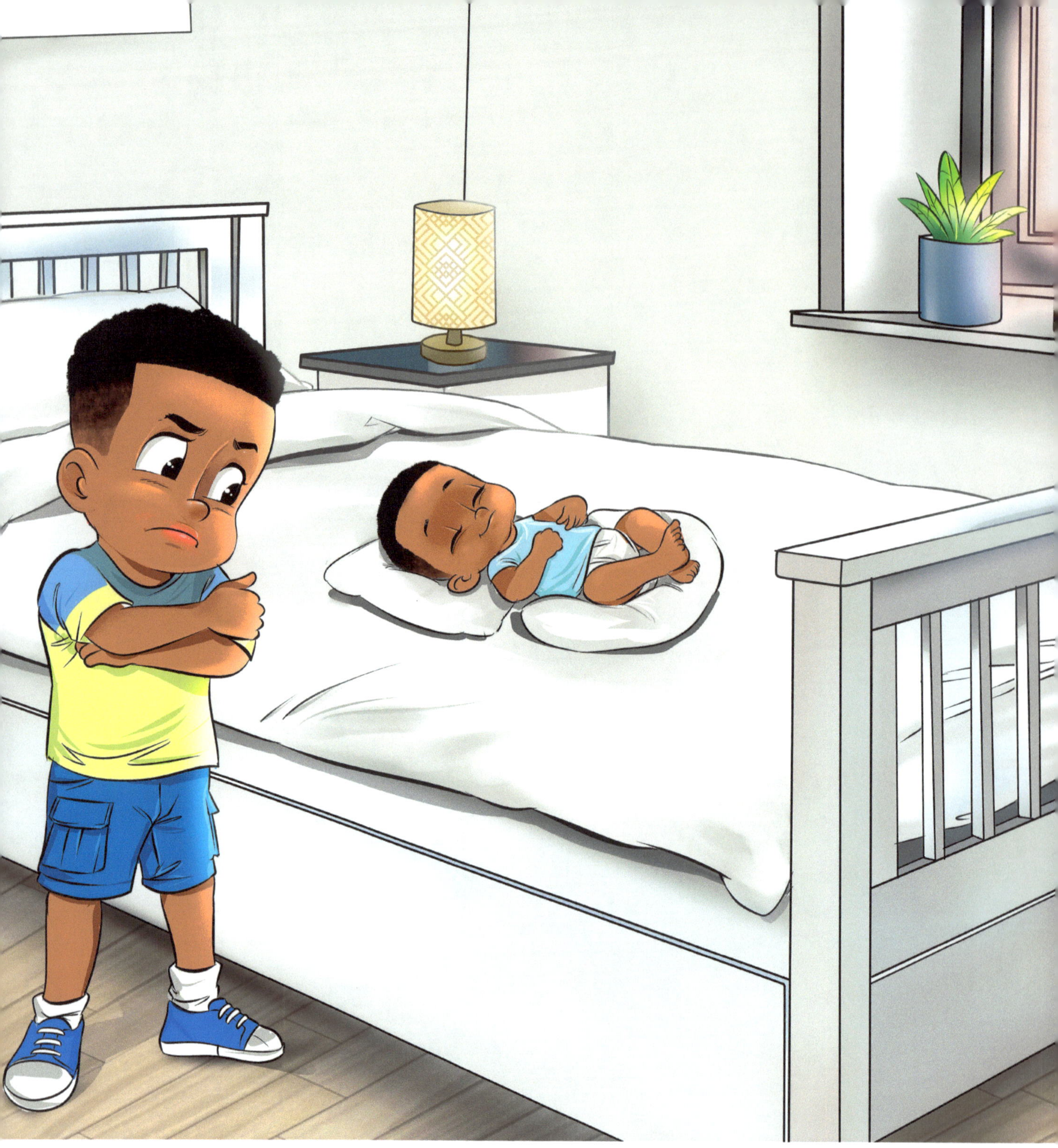

George can't do anything he wants to.

One day, George decides that he's had enough.

Baby brother has got to go.

George asks Mommy if they can take baby brother back to the hospital.
MOMMY SAYS, "NO."

George asks Daddy if baby brother can
live outside with the dog.
Daddy says, **"NO WAY."**

George even asks the postman if he can

post baby brother somewhere, but the

POSTMAN ONLY LAUGHS.

So, George decides that if baby brother won't leave,

HE WILL.

George will pack some clothes and his favorite toys.

Then he will join the circus or maybe live at the zoo.

Lions and zebras are **A LOT MORE FUN** than baby brothers.

George pulls up a bag,
BUT IT'S HEAVY.

He looks inside,

AND THERE IS A BOOK.

George opens the book and sees **BABY PICTURES.**

A baby held by Mommy and Daddy, a baby sleeping, a baby crying, a baby with curly hair just like him. There is even a photo of George's cousin playing with the baby.

These are photos of George as a baby.

Mommy sits next to George, and they look at the pictures together.

"Look at how small you were," says Mommy. "Then, when you grew bigger, your cousin showed you how to play and sing."

"I was really tiny," says George. "Just as tiny as baby brother is now."

"I wonder who will **TEACH BABY BROTHER** when he gets bigger," Mommy asks. "Who will show him how to play and sing?"

"Me," says George. "I will teach him how to
play, jump, sing and dance.
That's what **BIG BROTHERS** are for."

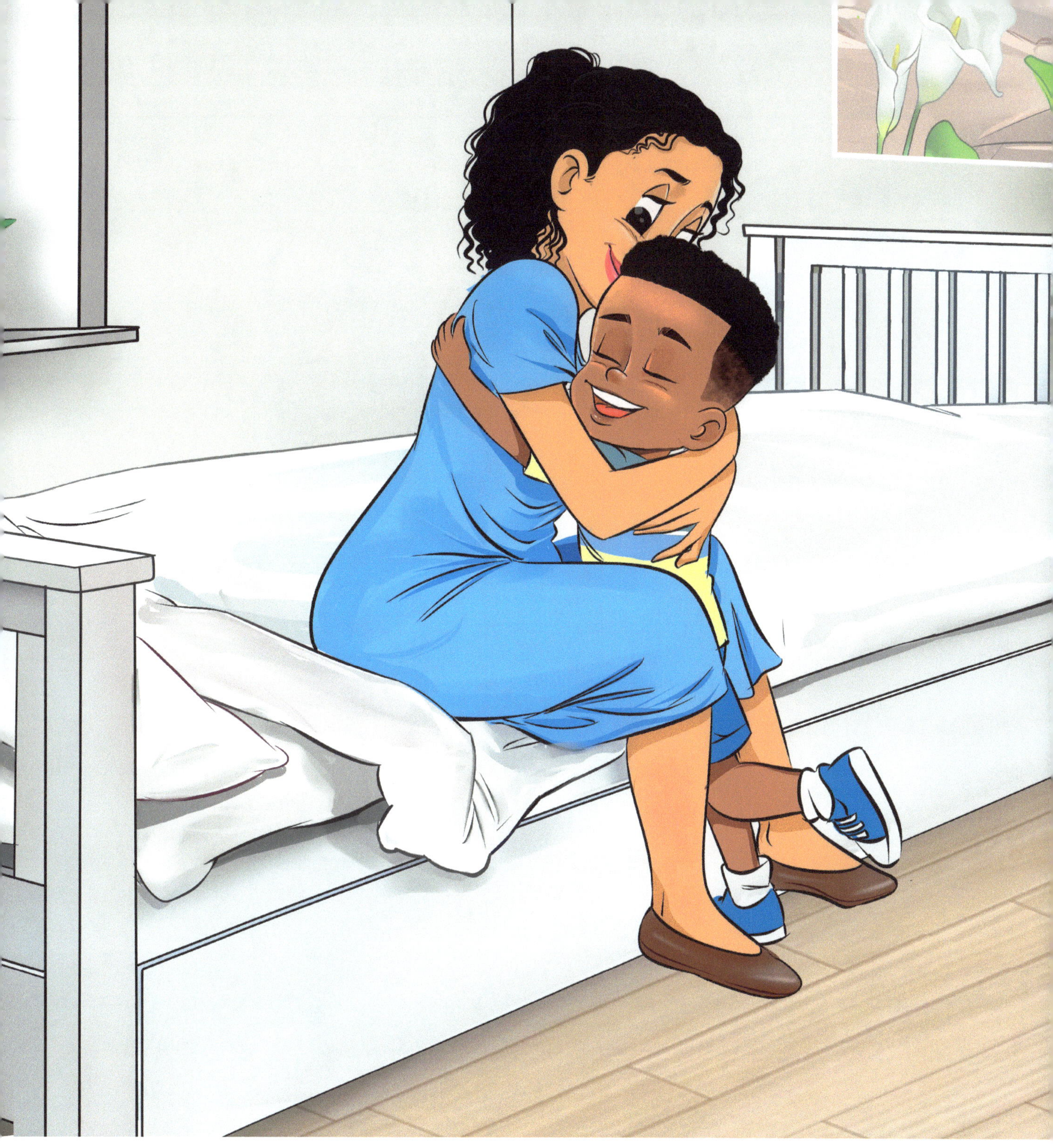

George hugs Mommy with a big smile,
AND MOMMY LAUGHS.

"MAYBE YOU NEED A BABY SISTER TOO."